NOTED

A JOURNAL TO EXPLORE HOW WE SHAPE, CREATE, AND DEVELOP IDEAS

ADAM TURNBULL

A Perigee Book

PERIGEE
An imprint of Penguin Random House LLC
375 Hudson Street, New York, New York 10014

NOTED

ISBN: 978-0-399-17352-3

First edition: October 2015

PRINTED IN THE UNITED STATES OF AMERICA

10 9 8 7 6 5 4 3 2 1

Most Perigee books are available at special quantity discounts for
bulk purchases for sales promotions, premiums, fund-raising, or educational use.
Special books, or book excerpts, can also be created to fit specific needs.
For details, write: SpecialMarkets@penguinrandomhouse.com.

NOTED

For Marianne & Stephen

Seeing blank spaces and finding ideas in different mediums can help lead you to new and unexpected places.

Take for instance a postcard. Does it make you think of a vacation? Or a friend? Or photographs? Or say, a letter. Does this make you think of your grandmother's handwriting? Receiving a check in the mail? Or the patterns inside your cell phone bill?

In the following pages, the open-ended prompts and images are meant to lead you to new ideas. Find your ideas in whatever way works best for you: Write in the book, don't write in it. Draw on the pages, don't draw on them. Think about things, don't think about things.

As you move from beginning to end, it's okay to add something or strike something out. Noted might be the place where you conceptualize your next business, jot down your ideas for a short film, or write a guest list for a party. Or you might simply flip through its pages for inspiration.

However you choose to use Noted, don't be precious with your ideas. Ideas aren't meant to be treated kindly. Ideas are messy—they should be built on, formed, shaped, and reinvented as they come to fruition. Use the blank spaces in front of you to collect ideas, drawings, thoughts, anything that is sparked in the moment looking at the page, and act on that inspiration because everything leads to something.

— Adam Turnbull

Take notes. Ask questions.

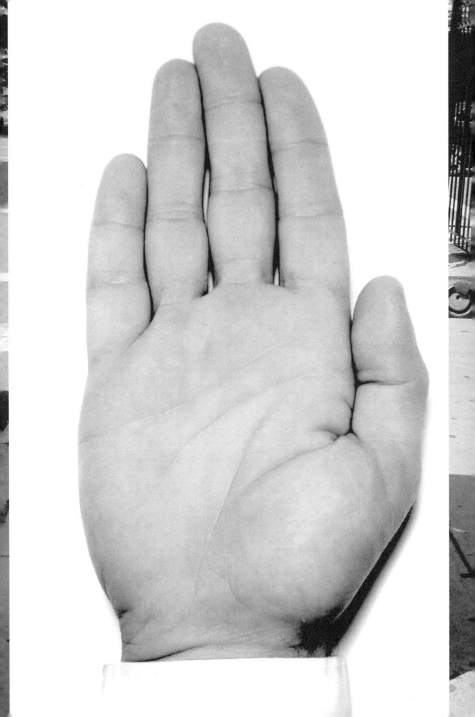

No idea is too good for a guest check.

Guest Check

SERVER	TABLE	GUESTS	CHECK NUMBER
			868600

TAX		
Thank You	TOTAL	

adams· 2100

Top ten?

The postcard was invented to boost the use of the postal service, encouraging people to keep things short and sweet.

~~rice~~ and Pole Fence

Starting a fire or a restaurant?

A card says 1,000 words.

PULL LEVER 14 - E
TO VOTE
OLIVE M. HANDW

VOT

7A

Your Vote & e
Greatly An

North Wh
Your Vote and Influence

Re-Elect

Gene Best

Marilyn Monroe wrote her most famous letters on hotel letterhead.

R. C. A.
RADIO
SPEAKER
IN EACH
ROOM

SEVEN FLOORS
EXCLUSIVELY FOR WOMEN
FIFTEEN FLOORS
FOR MEN AND WOMEN

Allerton Hotel

701 NORTH MICHIGAN AVENUE

Chicago

Richard Berry wrote the lyrics to "Louie, Louie" on toilet paper.

It's art if you say it is.

Which came first?

What for who?

From walls to canvas, anywhere is a good place to start.

Opportunity.

Old thoughts are as good as new ones.

xell **VHS** VIDEO CASSETTE

□ □SP (x1)   □LP (x2)   □EP (x3)

Insert this side into recorder   Do not

The start of something new.

Field trip!

Share some wisdom.

"It is good to have an end to journey toward; but it is the journey that matters, in the end."

– Ernest Hemingway

VAN life — is more
than a destination —
it is part of my Journey
to live simpler;
adventure, travel,
love. this is MY
JOURNEY!

Each day —
  Live simply.
  Reflect, Pray
  Connect
  Love
  Be grateful
  Move my body

That bingo moment!

A cork tree is harvested every 9 years;
all useful things take time.

Start a movement.
In the 1950s, the mail art movement
started, reimagining what
a canvas can be.

Make your own luck.

Murasaki Shikibu wrote the first novel, *The Tale of Genji*, in the 11th century.

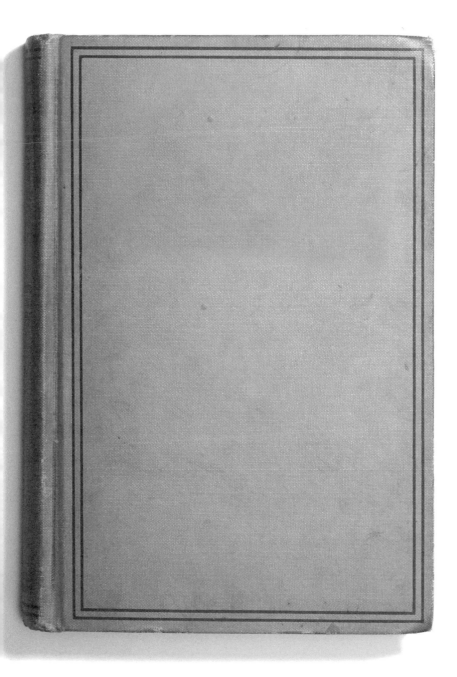

Learn.

Call a friend.

With all the money in the world?

Too much of anything and it will pop.

Limits are no issue. Where do you go?

Symmetry.
Nostalgia.
Detail.

A letter to…

There's always something to do.

TO-DO-LIST

Date:	Finished: ✔

TO-CALL-LIST

"Even a true artist does not always produce art."

– *Carroll O'Connor*

Plans for the first portable computer
were sketched on a napkin.

Imperfections
create perfection.

With the invention of the printing press
composers were able to print and distribute music.

Things we can't control.

**"FOR MOTION DISCOMFORT
AND
BABY DIAPER DISPOSAL"**

*Please place in waste receptacle
after use*

Not for toilet disposal

**Do not place in seat back
pocket after use**

Distractions.

 the *All Family* drink!

GIN RUMMY

WE	THEY		WE	THEY		WE	THEY	

"Fresh up" with *Seven-Up!*

BRIDGE SCORE SHEET ON THE OTHER SIDE

Winning isn't everything,
but it feels good.

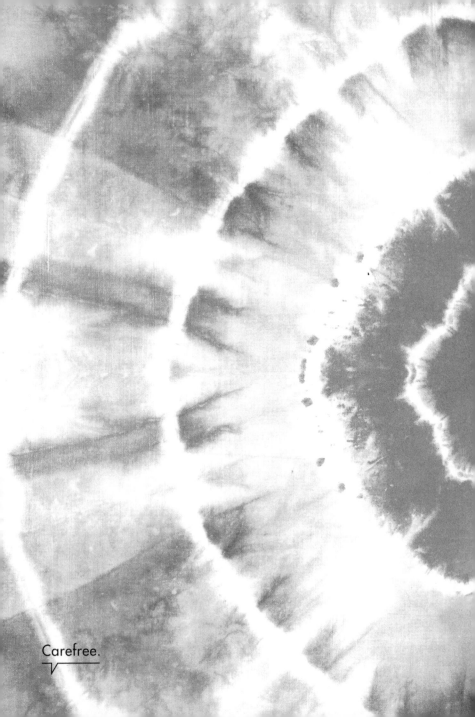

Carefree.

Everything has a price.

The ritual is as strong as the drink.

Beginning
or
end?

Your take on a classic.

Notes

What do you want this to be?

Make your mark.

"Travel makes one modest.
You see what a tiny place you
occupy in the world."

– *Gustave Flaubert*

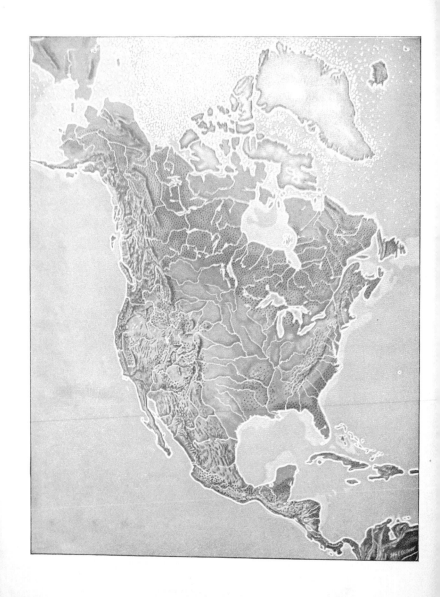

The bigger question is, What's inside?

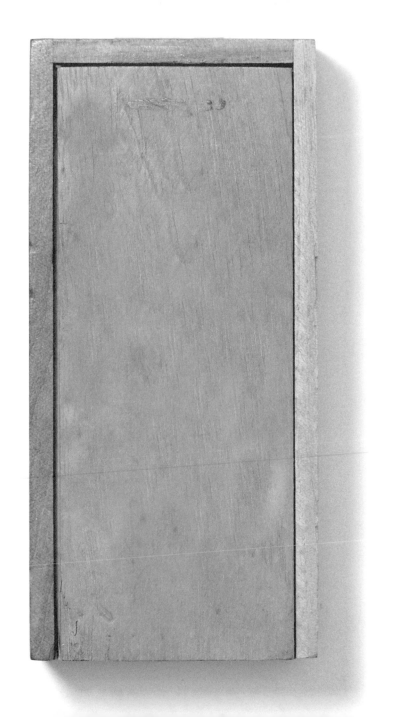

Mix tape!

| **A** DATE _____ · _____ ◯YES ◯NO | **B** DATE _____ · _____ ◯YES ◯NO |
| N.R. | N.R. |

Dust to dust.

This man deserves a hat.

JOHN G. B. ADAMS.
Sergeant-at-Arms, 1886 —

A fabric can define a culture.

Puzzled?

Iron out the creases.

To write is to start.

Small plans become big plans.

FEBRUARY, 1950

Thursday 2

Friday 3

Saturday 4

Memoranda

Change is as good as a vacation.

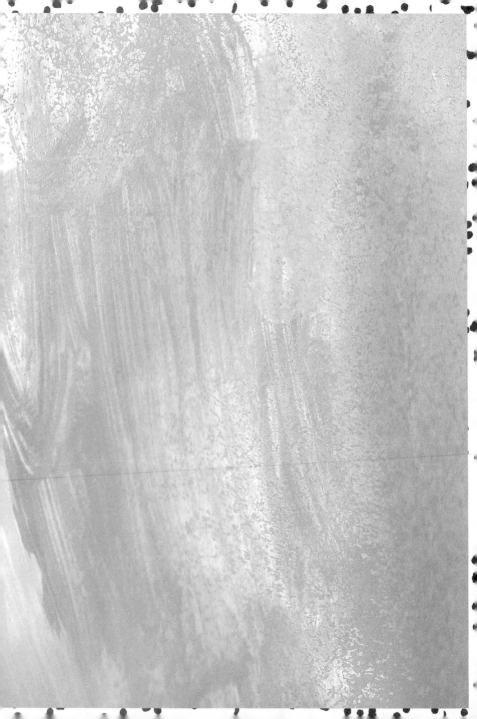

From where you
wish you were.

Ideas are far greater used in front of you.

Rethink.

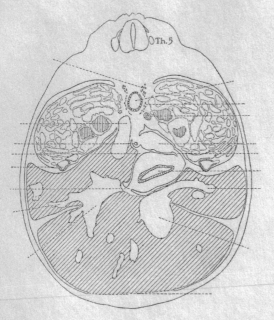

Th. 5

Section 24

75

Simplify the message.

The story of a found image.

Eating outside.

Nature or nurture?

"To act on a bad idea
is better than to not act at all."

– Nick Cave

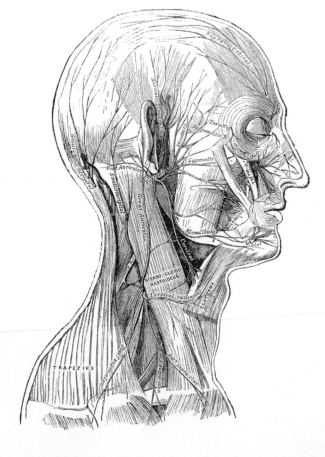

What's in front of you?

Something, anything!

IMPORTANT MESSAGE

FOR _____

DATE _____ TIME _____ A.M. P.M.

M _____

OF _____

PHONE/
CELL _____

TELEPHONED		PLEASE CALL	
CAME TO SEE YOU		WILL CALL AGAIN	
WANTS TO SEE YOU		RUSH	
RETURNED YOUR CALL		SPECIAL ATTENTION	

MESSAGE _____

_____

_____

_____

_____

_____

SIGNED _____

Life's precious moments.

Get off the grid...

The first consumer 5½-inch floppy disk
was made in 1976 and held 89.7 KB of data.

FILE 12

Visualizing a story will help you simplify it.

As good a surface as any.

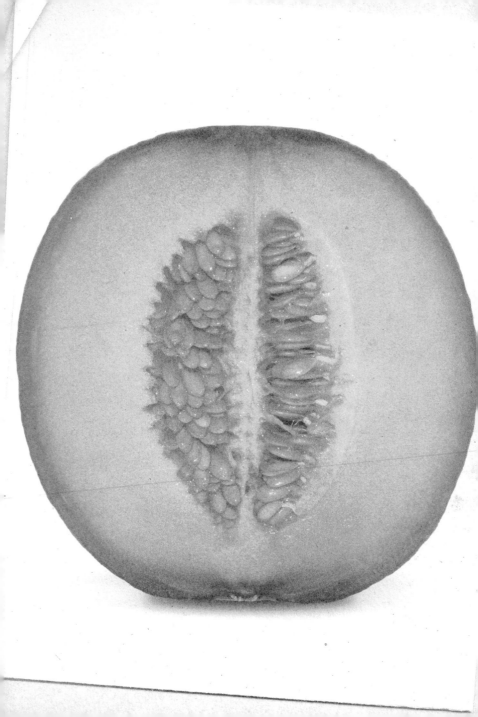

The kind of gesture that won't last...

The logo is as important as the taste.

NET 12 FL. OZ.

Each tells a different story.

Take it offline.

Acknowledgments

I would like to thank everyone I've ever met, especially the following:
Elizabeth Karp-Evans, Meg Leder, Alison Arden, John Duff, Ned Rogers,
Erez Horovitz, Alexander Singh, Lucy Munger, Ryan Ho, Kashi Sommers,
Nick Brinley, Michael Sharp, Edward Woodley, Melanie Topham,
and my all wonderful friends and family.

Adam Turnbull is an artist and designer based in New York. He divides his time between his art practice and Land-Line Studio, home to design, illustration, branding, digital, printed matter, and publishing projects. His experience working on many different projects in a variety of mediums allows him to keep ideas flowing—to not be limited by execution or resolution and to channel inspiration into art and design practices.

Adam has worked with clients such as Bloomberg Business, Cirque du Soleil, *Harvard Business Review*, Penguin Random House, and the *Washington Post*. He has exhibited art and design in Sydney, New York, London, Rome, Paris, and Montreal. In 2010, Adam was recognized by the Australian Graphic Design Association. In 2013, he received two honors from the Applied Arts Photography & Illustration Awards.

See more at adam-turnbull.com and land-line.com.